Zodiac Signs for Cross Stitch and Blackwork

Aquarius

Loretta Oliver

Copyright © 2017 Loretta Oliver & Stitching the Night Away

All rights reserved.

ISBN: 1546401873
ISBN-13: 978-1546401872

THANK YOU

I would like to take a moment to thank you for purchasing this pattern booklet, **I truly appreciate your support**.

Please visit **www.StitchingtheNightAway.com** to leave a comment or send me a photo of your finished projects to add to the gallery. I love seeing what people create with these patterns! It's beautiful to see how we can all start with the same pattern and come out with such unique finished projects.

CONTENTS

Aquarius	i
About These Patterns	iii
Version 1 – Cross Stitch Basic Aquarius Sign	1
Version 2 – Reverse Cross Stitch Zodiac Sign	3
Version 3 – Blackwork Outside, Cross Stitch Inside	5
Version 4 – Cross Stitch Outside, Blackwork Inside	7
Version 5 – Backstitch Outline Only	9
Project Ideas	11
About the Author	13

Aquarius ♒
January 19 – February 18

Trustworthy, creative, and intellectual, Aquarius is always brimming with great ideas and fun conversation, ever-willing to lend an ear or a helping hand.

The eleventh astrological sign in the Zodiac, originating from the constellation Aquarius. Symbolized by the Water-Bearer, though it's actually an Air sign.

Ruled by the unpredictable planet Uranus, Aquarius is the most eccentric zodiac sign — there's never a dull moment with an Aquarius around.

Friendly and future-minded, the humanitarians of the zodiac. The Water-Bearer represents community and mankind, and Aquarius is more concerned with the good of all than the good of one.

Birthstones: Amethyst, Garnet, Hematite, Amber

ABOUT THESE PATTERNS

You'll find that these patterns are without a floss legend or color key. That is because the idea here is to customize your own piece to your liking, using whatever floss colors you feel most drawn to at the time. If you're stitching a piece as a gift you might consider using the recipients favorite colors for stitching.

I've set the layout up to have patterns on one side of the paper throughout the book so that if you wish to mark things inside the book you'll have the space to do so and also to make scanning and copying out "working copies" a little bit easier to do for those that prefer not to mark their original copies.

This is your project and I want you to enjoy the process and come away with a piece that is as unique as you are.

Have fun and happy stitching!

VERSION 1 – CROSS STITCH BASIC AQUARIUS SIGN

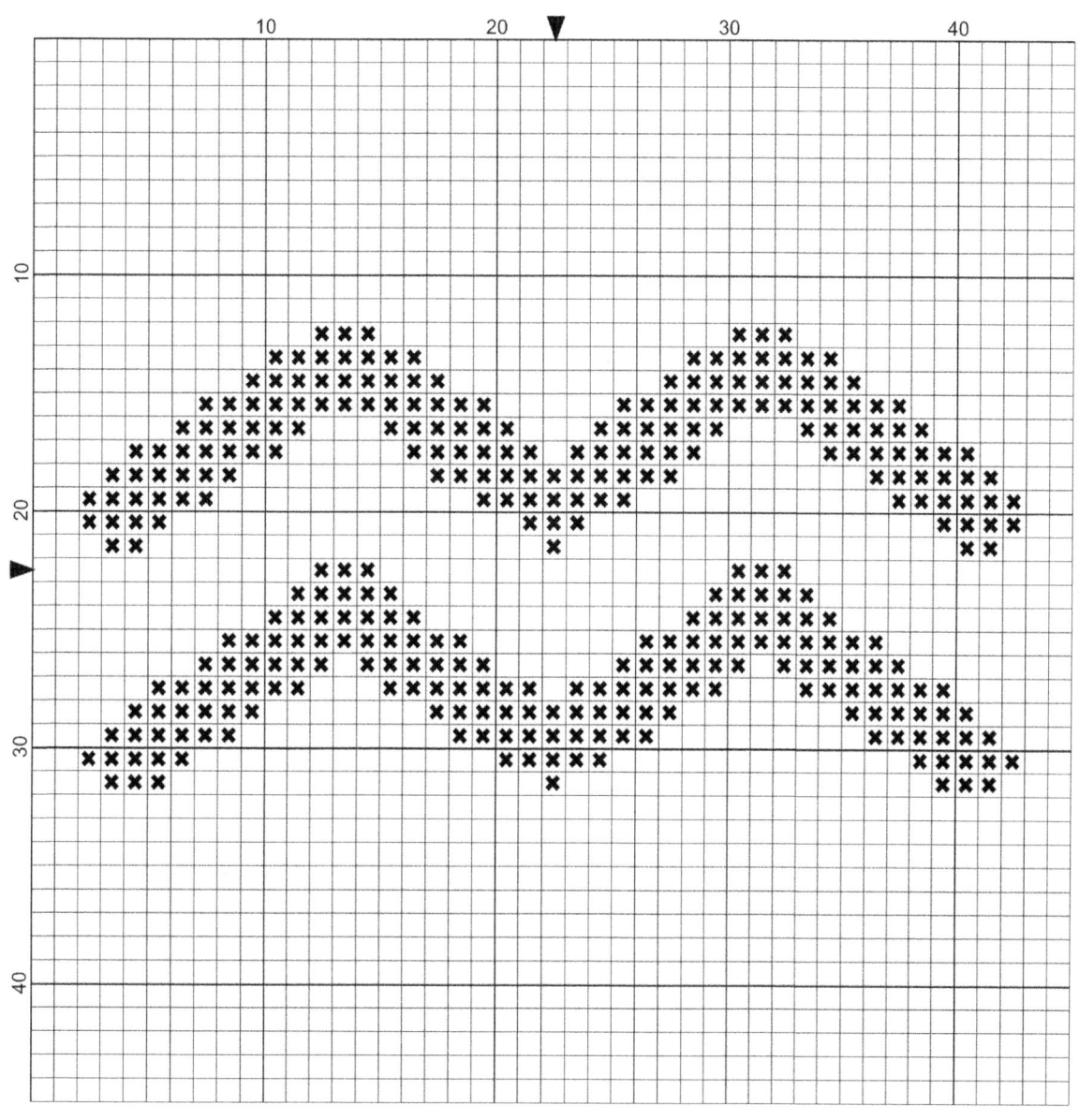

Zodiac Signs for Cross Stitching and Blackwork: Aquarius

VERSION 2 – REVERSE CROSS STITCH

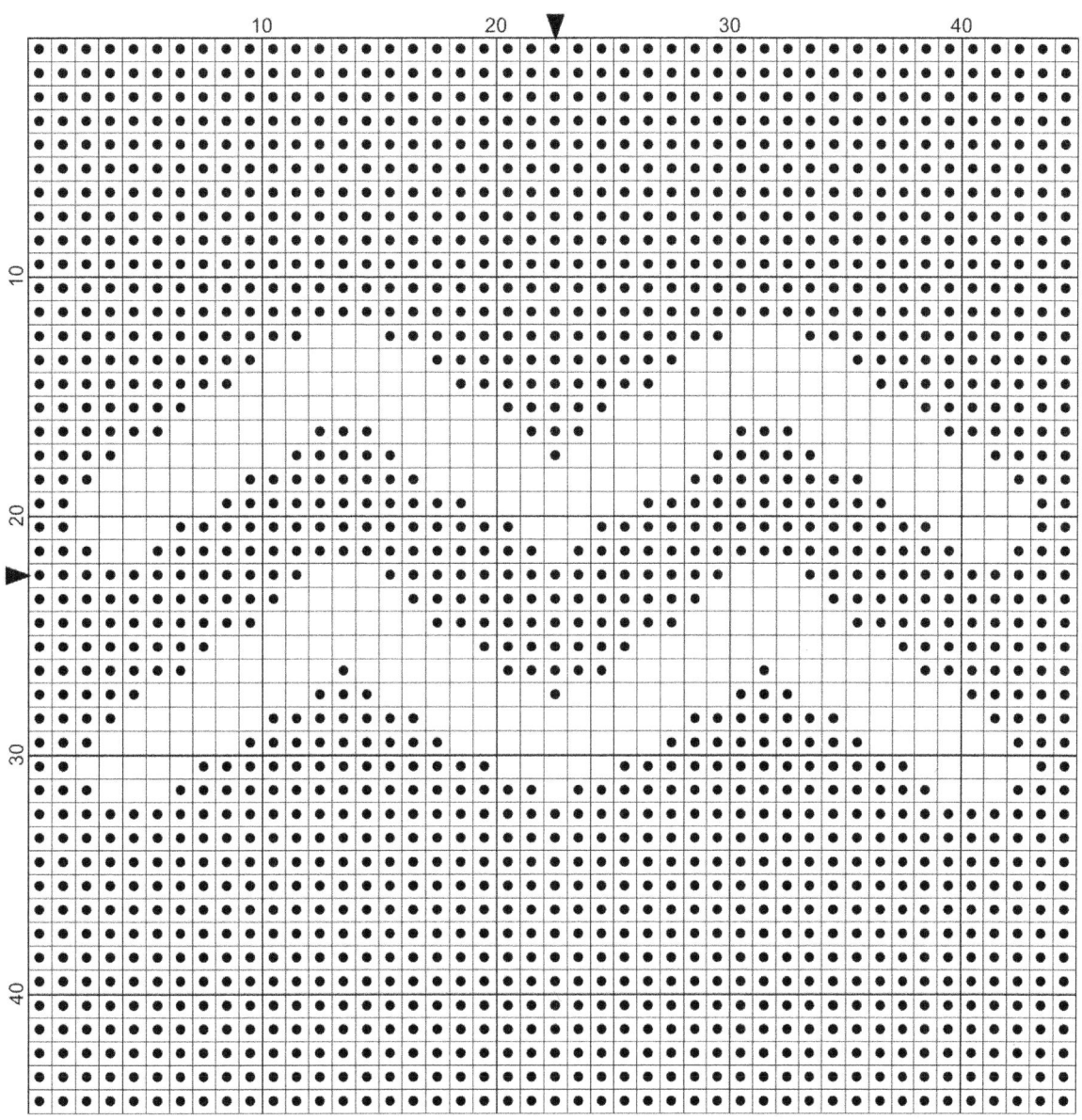

VERSION 3 – BLACKWORK OUTSIDE, CROSS STITCH INSIDE

VERSION 4 – CROSS STITCH OUTSIDE, BLACKWORK INSIDE

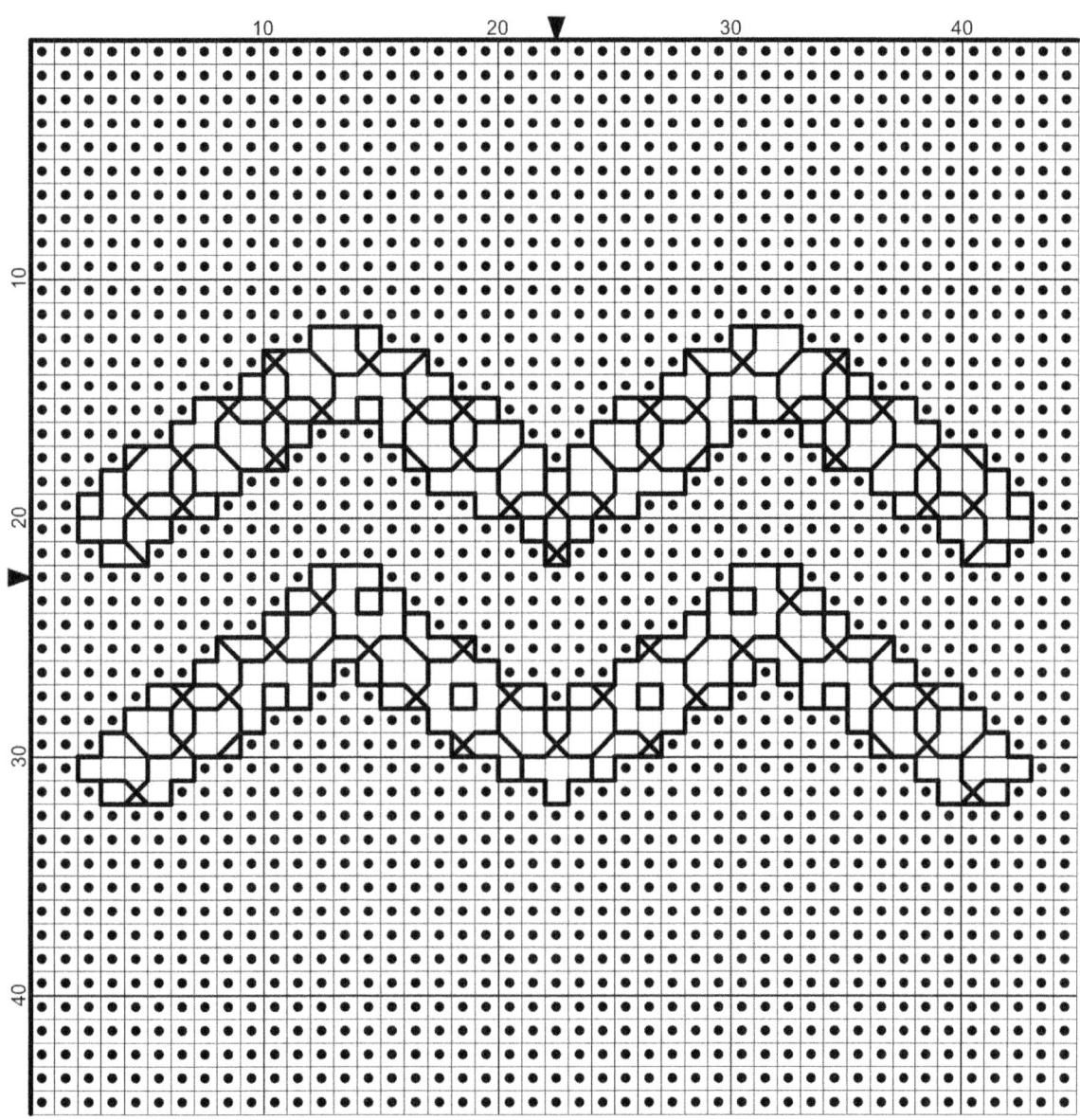

Zodiac Signs for Cross Stitching and Blackwork: Aquarius

VERSION 5 – OUTLINE ONLY

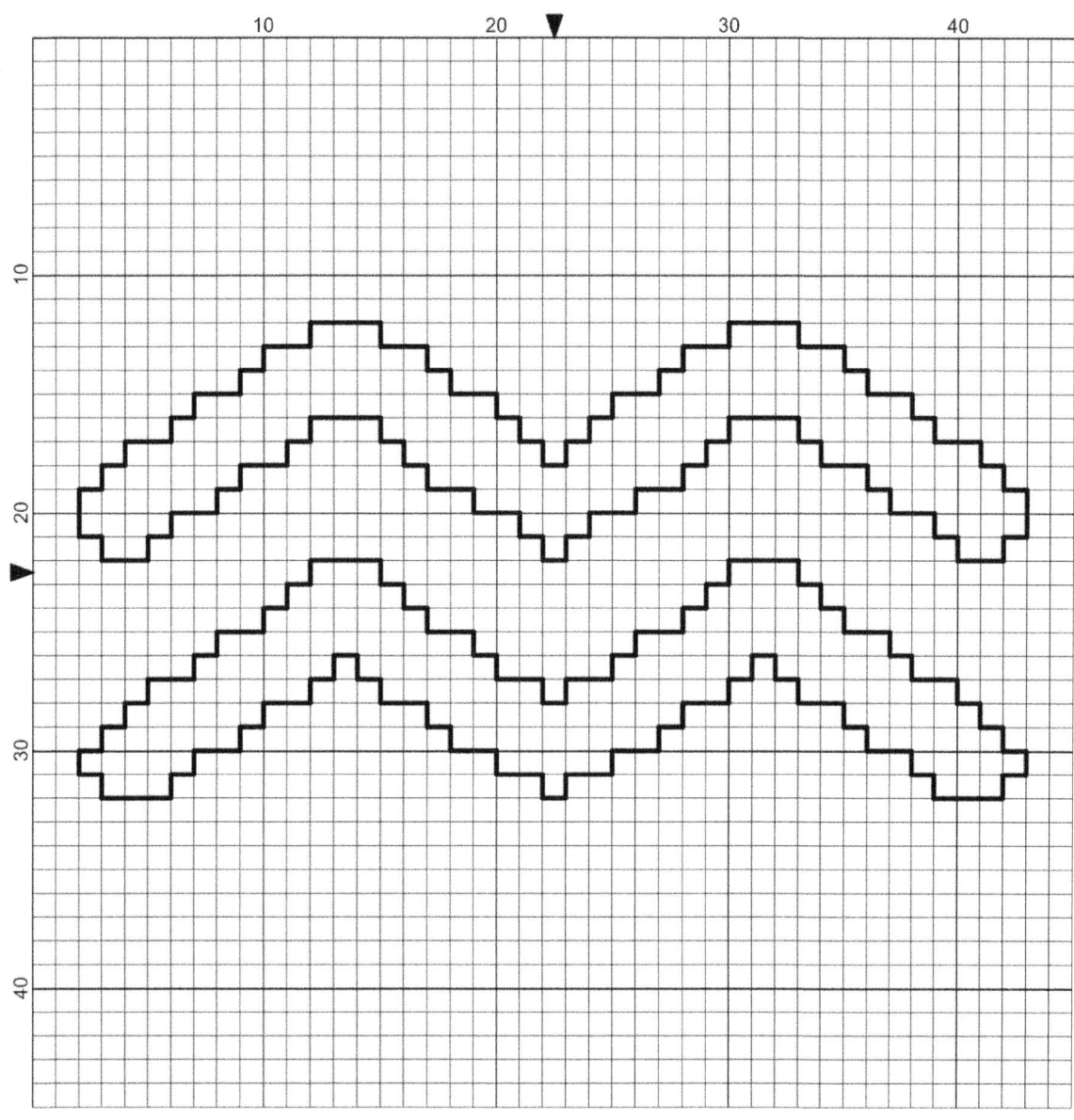

6 – A FEW PROJECT IDEAS

There are endless ways to use these designs and you're limited only by your imagination. Here are just a few fun ideas to get you started….

- Scented sachets

- Holiday ornaments

- Trinket boxes

- Pillows or throws

- Family zodiac sign samplers

- Wedding gifts

- Birthday gifts

Use these designs to customize just about anything with your zodiac signs. Have fun stitching and please do stop on over to share your projects with our community at www.StitchingtheNightAway.com/facebookgroup

ABOUT THE AUTHOR

Loretta Oliver has been publishing cross stitch patterns and information at StitchingtheNightAway.com since 2001 with a goal of sharing the joy of cross stitching with others worldwide.

Her first cross stitch project was when she was 8-years-old and a love of the fiber arts was born, she's been stitching ever since. When she came online she found a vast community of amazing stitchers and creative people to share the love of needlework with and found that connecting with those people made her love the hobby even more. Eventually growing a website and community, creating her own designs, and helping others learn to stitch and encouraging people to explore new stitching techniques, fun fibers, and new designs.

Find out more and connect with Loretta at www.StitchingtheNightAway.com

Printed in Great
Britain
by Amazon